Seventeenth-century English sampler; coloured silks on linen. Three fierce-looking boxers (see page 9) carrying sprays of foliage and glancing warily over their shoulders. The female figure which seems to have sprouted acorns is immediately recognisable by its splay feet.(Victoria and Albert Museum T217-1976)

SAMPLERS

Pamela Clabburn

Shire Publications Ltd

CONTENTS

Copyright © 1977 by Pamela Clabburn. First published 1977; reprinted 1980, 1981, 1983 and 1986. Shire Album 30. ISBN 0 85263 407 2.

Printed in Great Britain by C. I. Thomas & Sons (Haverfordwest) Ltd, Press Buildings, Merlins Bridge, Haverfordwest, Dyfed.

COVER: *Sampler made to commemorate the Emancipation Act of 1833, which gradually abolished slavery in the colonies. It is one of the many samplers where the worker has later unpicked her age, leaving only the date. (Reproduced by kind permission of Mrs S. G. Allen.)*

BELOW: *English sampler, 1821; signed 'Hannah Bowlin' and dated, red silk on linen. However brilliant and precocious the child it does not seem possible that Hannah Bowlin could have worked this at the age of six. There is nothing childlike about it, and the perfection of the cross stitch on the very fine linen must surely be the work of an adult, or at least a much older sister. (Norfolk Museums Service, Strangers Hall Museum 191.946.1.) (See Gift Samplers and Puzzles, page 14.)*

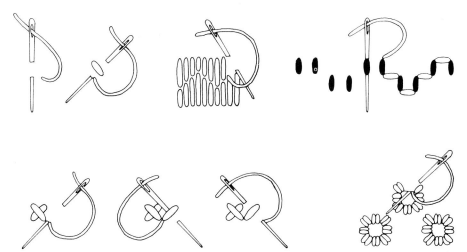

Stitches for samplers: (top row, from left) single cross, black satin, Holbein; (bottom row, from left) marking stitches, Algerian eye.

INTRODUCTION

Samplers were a necessary rather than a merely ornamental product of the sixteenth century, and though there are none still known to be in existence from the early part of the century, from 1502 onwards they are often mentioned in wills and inventories. The first book was not printed in England until 1477 when Caxton started his press at Westminster, so until then there could be no printed designs for needlewomen to follow. Instead the worker took a narrow piece of linen and on it recorded the patterns she had seen used by other people, or the patterns she had used herself, adding to them from time to time and probably passing them on to her daughters, who would also use them. These pieces of linen were called samplers or examplers from the French *essamplaire,* which means any kind of work to be copied or imitated.

During the sixteenth century books became more common and the first pattern book was printed at Augsburg in 1523. Others followed from France, Italy and England and by the end of the century there were enough books of designs to make the sampler as a record of pattern unnecessary. But samplers had another use – they were admirable vehicles for teaching children the different techniques of sewing which they would need when they were grown up, and for three hundred and fifty years they have been used to teach the marking and darning of household linen (darning samplers), the making of dresses and underwear (plain sewing samplers), as well as to teach geography (map samplers), and record family joys and sorrows and all kinds of domestic trivia. They were also used to inculcate filial obedience together with moral virtues and resignation to the will of God, and there are few samplers of the eighteenth and nineteenth centuries which do not contain at least one moral verse or precept.

The seventeenth-century sampler was usually long and narrow and either band, spot or random in design, worked in natural-coloured linen or silk thread, or in many coloured silks. The band samplers of the early part of the century were often of cutwork, which includes darning on a netted foundation (*lacis*), and buttonholing round raw edges when threads have been cut away and then making a design with rows of buttonhole stitch (*reticella*). They were also worked in bands showing the use of various stitches such as Holbein or double-running, block satin, cross or Algerian eye. Other samplers of the seventeenth century are more informal with small isolated patterns jotted down on the linen as we would jot small sketches in a notebook. Some pieces of needlework of this date consist of rows of motifs and look like samplers, but these motifs were meant to be cut out and applied to other pieces of work.

The eighteenth-century sampler ceased to be long and became square, generally with a border, a verse and many little motifs such as trees, houses and birds. One of the most common of these motifs was the crown or coronet. These are found on numberless samplers, usually showing the entire range from a king's crown to the coronet of a baron, often with the appropriate letter, K, D, M, E, V, L or B, to remind the worker which was which. These coronets would be used to mark the linen and underwear belonging to the nobility, and though to some children they were just an attractive motif, to others they would be a necessity for their later work as lady's or sewing maid.

By the nineteenth century individuality was being stifled and as the century progressed samplers became more and more stereotyped until by the end they were little more than repetitive schoolgirl exercises. The designs became increasingly alike, with most of the motifs taken from the many pattern books of the time. Occasionally a sampler can be found which has charm and originality but on the whole those dating from about 1850 to 1900 are dull to the point of boredom. One innovation of interest was the plain sewing sampler. The nineteenth century was the era of large quantities of cotton and flannel underwear, enormous trousseaux and many cotton, linen and muslin accessories. Men's shirts and nightshirts were often made in the home, and the processes and stitches involved in the making and mending of these garments were all practised on samplers. Some schools, such as the Kildare Model School at Dublin, printed their own instruction books with a blank page left for the worked specimen, and these would be for the children to copy. When the City and Guilds examinations started in the last part of the century plain sewing samplers were included in the needlework syllabus and there are many still to be found, beautifully worked and interesting today as a reminder of skills which are now virtually forgotten.

At the end of the nineteenth century it might have been thought that the era of samplers was over and that with the advent of traced designs, many needlework magazines and the domestic sewing machine there would be no further use for small patterns, linen marking and plain sewing processes. This was true, but with the revival of interest in all forms of arts and crafts and better teaching a new type of sampler came into use. This paid less attention to pattern and more to stitches, their capabilities and their possibilities. Some samplers might consist mainly of rows of stitches worked in different threads, while others became decorative panels exploiting a single stitch or group of stitches to make a complete design. These must still be called samplers as they are for use and reference and fulfil the original definition of a work to be copied or imitated, but more than anything else some of them have a charm and skill which make them minor works of art and make it certain that the art of sampler-making will continue for many years.

CUTWORK SAMPLERS

Many cutwork samplers were worked in the seventeenth century and probably also in the sixteenth, though few of the latter have survived. They are mostly worked on narrow linen with the length of the sampler representing the width of the woven fabric, and in nearly all cases they consist of border patterns and single motifs taken from the pattern books of the time. Many of the designs from these samplers were worked on the lace collars, cuffs and handkerchiefs so widely worn by both men and women in this century.

BELOW LEFT: 1649; signed 'SID' and dated; linen thread on linen. A sampler typical of so many in the seventeenth century. The designs are built up of rows of buttonholing, each row being worked into the previous row, the same technique as that for needlepoint lace. The top line shows the angel appearing to Abraham and Sarah. Other motifs are the acorn, S shape and mermaid. (Victoria and Albert Museum T115-1956)

BELOW RIGHT: Mid seventeenth century; English; linen thread on linen. This sampler is particularly interesting because it is unfinished and still has its original vellum tacked on at the back of the top line. This shows how the linen was held rigid when the threads were withdrawn and the pattern built up. (Norfolk Museums Service, Strangers Hall Museum 135.22)

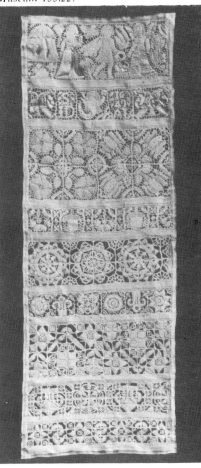
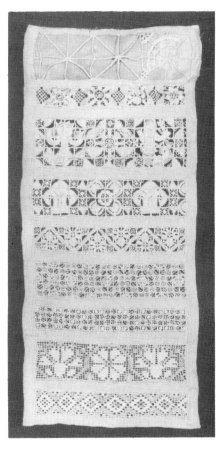

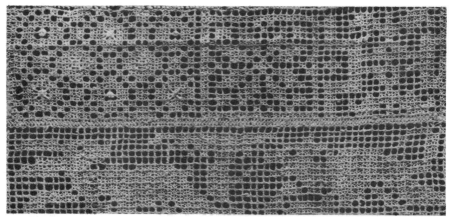

ABOVE: *Mid seventeenth century; English; linen thread on linen. Detail of sampler with drawn thread work, the pattern made by interlacing threads round the overcast bars and across the holes. (Victoria and Albert Museum 742-99)*

BELOW LEFT: *1699-1700; English; signed 'Susanna Wilkinson' and dated; coloured silks and linen thread on linen. This sampler shows both the formal schoolgirl exercise of alphabets and numerals and superbly executed cutwork and hollie point. The alphabets and numerals at the top are worked in geometrical satin stitch and Algerian eye stitch, the numerals at the bottom in cross stitch and the crowns in double running stitch. (Fitzwilliam Museum, Cambridge T20-1938)*

BELOW RIGHT: *1647; English; signed 'A. Nodo' and dated; coloured silks and white linen thread on linen. Detail of a typical band sampler which includes some border patterns in white work as well as those in coloured silks. The little acorn patterns and others in double running stitch and black work must be considered rather old-fashioned by 1647. (Victoria and Albert Museum 751-1902)*

6

BAND SAMPLERS

Prevalent in the seventeenth century and probably earlier, band samplers, in coloured silks on linen, generally show border patterns which would be for use on costume and domestic linens. The designs are always rather dense with few spaces, as was the fashion in Stuart embroidery.

ABOVE: *Mid seventeenth century; English; coloured silks on linen. Mostly border patterns with one section of small spot motifs. Two designs have the patterns in reserve in the technique usually known as Assisi work. (Victoria and Albert Museum 516A-1877)*

RIGHT: *Second half of the seventeenth century; English; coloured silks on linen. Band sampler with the borders interspaced with the lines of a poem. Curiously the lettering is upside-down in relation to the designs. Little attention is paid to the spacing of the words with the last letter of a word often starting the next line. (Victoria and Albert Museum 480-1894)*

RANDOM SAMPLERS

Random samplers appear chiefly in the seventeenth and sometimes in the nineteenth century and represent what might be called 'try-outs' in different techniques and threads together with odd patterns noted for reference. The layout can be formal but is more likely to be haphazard. In the nineteenth century these samplers were worked on long strips of canvas bound at the edges with ribbon; they were rolled up and kept in the workbox for reference.

BELOW LEFT: *Early to mid seventeenth century; English; coloured silks and metal thread on linen. This sampler has obviously been used to try out stitches and patterns and the needle marks show evidence of much unpicking. The drawing of the design is clearly seen in the unfinished slips of rose and carnation. (Fitzwilliam Museum, Cambridge T3-1928)*

BELOW RIGHT: *Mid seventeenth century; English; coloured silks on linen. Sampler showing different methods of arranging motifs into patterns. Most of these are designed as all-over patterns rather than the more usual borders and nearly all are worked in rococo stitch. (Victoria and Albert Museum T262-1927)*

Seventeenth century; English; coloured silks on linen. Two boxers carrying heart-shaped flowers. The acorn (?), which looks rather like a wing, probably derives from foliage behind the figure. (Victoria and Albert Museum 829-1902)

SAMPLERS WITH BOXERS

In the seventeenth and early eighteenth centuries many of the coloured band samplers were worked with one line of the pattern consisting of small male figures looking sideways but walking forwards towards a large plant or shrub. The figures are sometimes naked, worked only in outline, and sometimes dressed in very modern-looking 'shorts and sweater' with bobbed hair. They always carry in one hand an unrecognisable object resembling a flower, a spray or a heart. Their attitude with one leg forward and one arm up holding the object looks rather as though they were about to fight and so the modern term for them is *boxers*. They derive, however, from a motif common all over the Continent in the sixteenth and seventeenth centuries of a lover and his beloved exchanging gifts. In the English samplers the beloved has changed into a shrub or tree which can still be seen to have a head, body, two arms and two feet, and to which the lover forever offers gifts. (See also illustration on page 1.)

LEFT: 1706; English; signed 'Ann Edwards' and dated; coloured silks on linen. Three boxers strongly resembling small boys of the 1920s. The female figure between them is still recognisable even though it has become a stylised tree. (Fitzwilliam Museum, Cambridge T102-28)

9

HOLLIE POINT SAMPLERS

Hollie point samplers were frequently made in the eighteenth century, when hollie point insertions were used in babies' gowns, caps and first shirts. The technique is that of needlepoint lace in so far as it consists of rows of buttonhole stitch, the stitches in each row going between the stitches in the previous row, but the pattern is made by omitting stitches and so consists of a series of tiny holes which show up dark. The designs are very simple, consisting of stylised flowers, geometrical patterns, names, dates and mottoes such as 'sweet baby'.

BELOW: 1737; English; signed 'SB' and dated; linen thread on linen. Hollie point and drawn thread motifs, both large and small with borders of geometrical satin stitch. (Fitzwilliam Museum, Cambridge T137-1928)

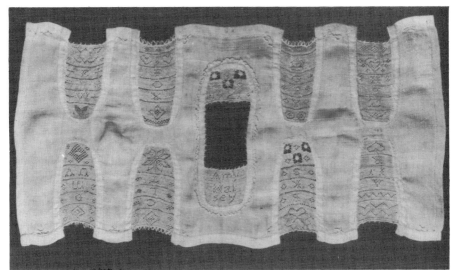

ABOVE: *1741; English; signed 'Amy Malsey' and dated; linen thread on fine linen.*
BELOW: *1791; English; signed 'Ann Blake' and dated; linen thread on fine linen mounted on pink satin. Taken together these two samplers are interesting in that they show how long-lived this style was and how little it varied. Both incorporate a small amount of drawn work and the same type of geometrical design with crowns and hearts; it is tempting, though probably unwise, to imagine that Ann Blake might have used Amy Malsey's sampler as a guide. (Norfolk Museums Service, Strangers Hall Museum 102.928 and 000.000)*

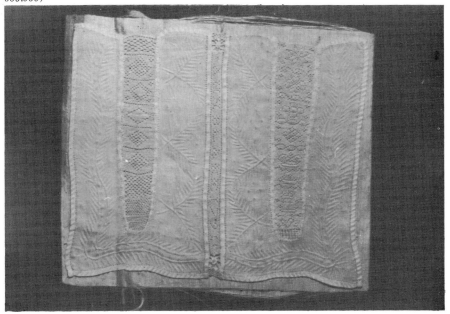

SCHOOL SAMPLERS

Many samplers of the eighteenth and nineteenth centuries were worked in schools of one type or another – dame schools, academies, orphanages, village or charity schools – and a number of these have the name and even the address of the establishment on the sampler. In a number of cases it is only through discovering a sampler with this information that the social historian knows that there was a school in a particular place, and this gives the sampler added interest. Sometimes the sampler also included the name of the teacher, which probably acted as a testimonial.

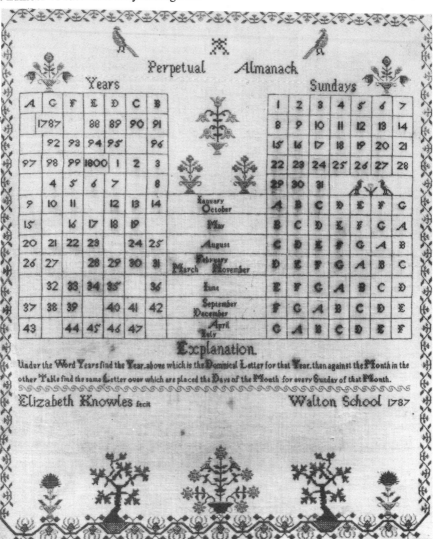

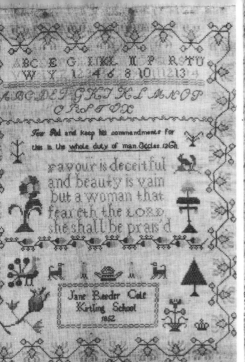

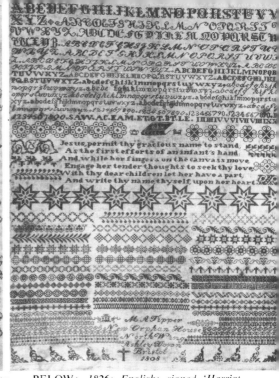

ABOVE: 1852; English; signed 'Jane Reeder Cole, Kirtling School' and dated; coloured silks on linen scrim. The Workwoman's Guide of 1837 says that the upright alphabet was most commonly used, while the Italian or sloping letters were for use on fine linen such as handkerchiefs. The conservatism of samplers is shown by the honeysuckle border on this specimen which was also worked on the samplers of 1826 (below) and 1787 (opposite). (Fitzwilliam Museum, Cambridge T7-1943)

ABOVE RIGHT: 1808; English; signed 'M. A. Tipper New Orphan House North Wing Ashley Down Bristol' and dated; red and black thread on linen. One of the many samplers still to be found from the Bristol orphanages. Here no corner of the linen has been wasted, and there are many alphabets, numerals and border patterns, all worked in cross stitch. Most of these children would go into service and one of their jobs might be to mark the household linen; hence the need for a high standard of workmanship and the necessity to learn as many varieties of lettering as possible.(Fitzwilliam Museum, Cambridge T11-1952)

OPPOSITE: 1787; English; signed 'Elizabeth Knowles' and dated; Walton School; coloured silks on linen. This perpetual almanack shows that the school must have had a very high standard of needlework or else Elizabeth was a star pupil, in which case her skill probably drew other pupils to the school. (Victoria and Albert Museum T75-1925)

BELOW: 1826; English; signed 'Harriet Jones Wrought this at Mrs Almgills School High Street Bewdley' and dated; coloured silks on linen. Houses which appear as motifs on samplers may occasionally represent the home or the school of the worker, but more often they come from one of the many pattern books in use. (Bewdley Museum)

GIFT SAMPLERS AND PUZZLES

Some samplers were made as gifts to friends and others were so valued that they were left as bequests in wills. Others might be birthday presents and in many cases this is stated on the inscription. However there is some evidence to suggest caution regarding the name on a sampler. If the wording says, for example, 'Mary Smith, her work' or 'Mary Smith wrought this', then obviously the sampler is the work of Mary Smith. If, on the other hand, there is only the name with, possibly, the age there is a chance, though we may never know for certain, that the sampler was worked for the child rather than by the child. The worker could have been a relation who worked it as a birthday present, or possibly it was worked for the child to copy.

ABOVE: *1598; English; signed 'Jane Bostocke' and dated; coloured silks and seed pearls on linen. This enchanting sampler has the distinction of being the earliest one known which is dated and was, as the inscription says, worked for two-year-old Alice Lee by Jane Bostocke, possibly her godmother, aunt, sister or mother. We shall never know which. The top part is full of animals to delight a child, including a dog carrying its lead, a chained bear, a deer and a lively terrier named Juno, while the rest is filled with patterns with stylised flowers and fruits, including grapes and the much-loved strawberry. (Victoria and Albert Museum T190-1960)*

OPPOSITE: *1833/4; signed 'Martha Grant' and dated; coloured silks on linen scrim. This sampler is a puzzle. If Martha Grant worked it aged ten years she could hardly have foretold her death at the age of eleven. If she started it and left it unfinished, what was she going to put into the second cartouche? The most careful search cannot find any difference in technique. But certainly Martha Grant did not work all of it if she worked any of it. (Norfolk Museums Service, Strangers Hall Museum 215.954.2)*

15

DARNING SAMPLERS

In the late eighteenth century and again in the early twentieth century the darning sampler became very common. It was geared to the teaching of exquisitely fine plain sewing in schools and the darning of the muslin dresses which were universally worn at the earlier date, while later it helped to teach children to darn more prosaic stockings and woollens. The darns were worked by the counted thread, and while some had holes cut out which were then filled with very neat work the majority consisted of crosses making an interesting pattern where the two arms met.

BELOW LEFT: *1784; English; signed 'Esther Anne Smith' and dated; coloured silks on linen. Five crosses and three half crosses in different patterns. For some reason Esther Anne has left the ends of her arms very ragged and this takes away from the neatness and skill of the darns. (Norfolk Museums Service, Strangers Hall Museum)* BELOW RIGHT: *1901; English; wool on wool. Part of the City and Guilds final examination in needlework for 1901. Darning remained an essential skill until after the Second World War and it was a prerequisite of any needlework examination. (Norfolk Museums Service, Strangers Hall Museum 366.971)*

MAP SAMPLERS

At the end of the eighteenth century and the beginning of the nineteenth it was the practice in schools to combine the teaching of geography with that of needlework. As a result there are a great number of beautifully executed map samplers to be found. These vary in content from a small district or county through a country to a continent, and even, in the case of globe samplers, the world.

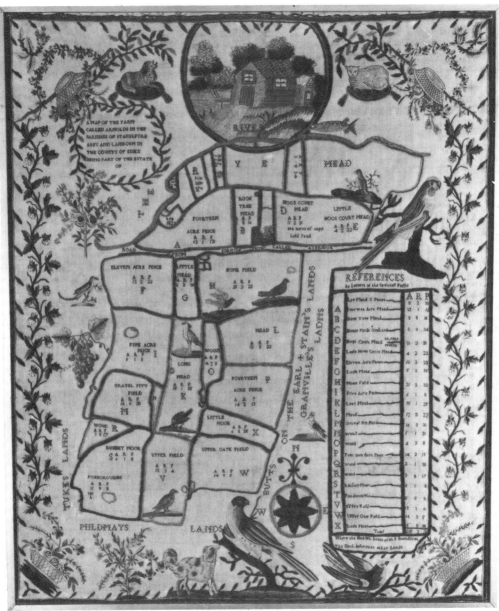

Late eighteenth century; English; coloured silks on woollen canvas. 'A Map of the Farm called Arnolds in the parishes of Stapleford Abby and Lambourn in the County of Essex being part of the estate of . . .' and unfortunately the name of the farm's owner has not been included though all the owners abutting are named. This is a fascinating piece of work and obviously a labour of love with all the local birds and domestic pets included. (Victoria and Albert Museum T65-1954)

17

OPPOSITE: *1797; English; signed 'Elizabeth Hawkins' and dated; silk on linen and silk. In common with a number of maps that include a lot of sea a dark green silk has been put under the fine linen; this makes the seas appear dark and the land stand out clearly. The countries are outlined in three or four rows of cross stitch. Needlework maps are seldom very accurate geographically and place names are often put wherever they will fit in rather than exactly where they should be. (Victoria and Albert Museum T165-1959)*

LEFT: *1800; English; signed 'A. Cooper' and dated; silk and chenille threads on linen. Map of England with the counties outlined with three rows of chenille while the lettering is worked in cross stitch and Algerian eye stitch. (Collection A. Snowdon)*

BELOW: *Early nineteenth century; English; signed 'Eliza Sophia Newton Pupil Teacher 1st yr'; coloured silks on linen. Map of Norfolk showing the county divided into hundreds, the figures tallying almost exactly with the key on Cooper's map of Norfolk of 1808. The puzzle of this map is to discover what the symbols in several of the hundreds represent. They are all worked to the same design and resemble a globe with handles mounted on a tripod. It is suggested that they might represent beacons placed in readiness for the expected invasion of Napoleon. This map is unusual in that it is signed by a pupil teacher and so perhaps was for the children to copy. (Norfolk Museums Service, Strangers Hall Museum 541.975)*

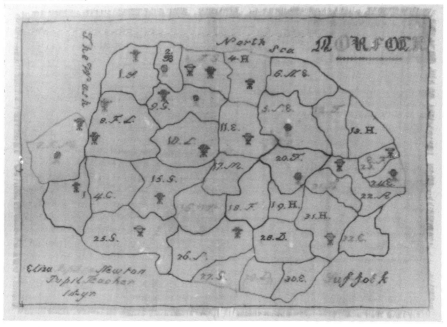

18

RELIGIOUS SAMPLERS

A great number of samplers include a religious or moral verse, which might be part of a hymn or a few lines from a psalm. Some go further than this and inscribe the whole of the Creed, the Lord's Prayer or the Commandments, making certain that the child knew the essential truths by heart.

RIGHT: *1868; English; signed 'Susanna Roberts' and dated; coloured silks on linen. Another type of religious sampler using the rebus, or pictures instead of words. The left-hand side reads 'The Cross is my Anchor, No Cross No Crown. God is my Shield'; and the right-hand side 'The Cross is my Anchor, No Cross No Crown, No Thorns No Crown'. (Norfolk Museums Service, Strangers Hall Museum 333.965)*

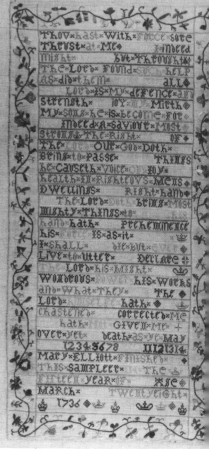

ABOVE LEFT: *1842; English; signed 'Ellen Churchill' and dated; blue silk on canvas. Very much a plain village-school sampler with no embellishments but the crowns. Ellen would almost certainly be going into service. (Norfolk Museums Service, Strangers Hall Museum 151.949.3)* ABOVE RIGHT: *1736; English; signed 'Mary Elliott' and dated; coloured silks on linen. Mary Elliott has taken great pains to fit her rather depressing poem into lines but has been completely arbitrary in her choice of capitals or lower-case letters within each word. (Victoria and Albert Museum T22-1940)*

FAMILY OCCASIONS

Samplers have been used to commemorate all kinds of family happenings from the early eighteenth century onwards, but by far the greatest number of this type occur in the nineteenth century. In some cases they seem to have been worked for a permanent record, while in others the child has been set her sampler of mourning as an expression of piety.

OPPOSITE: *First half of the nineteenth century; English; signed 'S. Stearn'; coloured silks on linen canvas. A record of the marriage and children of Thomas and Elizabeth Markham. This may have been intended for use by later generations in the same way as writing in the family Bible. It is tantalising not knowing the relationship of S. Stearn. She might have been Susan or Sarah working the sampler after her marriage, but was more likely to have been a nurse or governess. (Victoria and Albert Museum T94-1939)*

Thomas Markham   Elizabeth Boldero

Son of   Daughter of

William & Mary   Simon & Elizabeth

Markham   Boldero

Their Children   in   Maried in the Year   1824 to   Rotation of Birth

Thomas Markham
Born Septr 23rd 1826

Susan S Markham
Born Novr 27th 1827

Sarah E Markham
Born Jan^{ry} 15th 1829

Mary Ann Markham
Born June 13th 1830

Caroline Markham
Born Jan^{ry} 18th 1832

Thomas Markham
Born June 14th 1833

Charles H Markham
Born Septr 26th 1834

Elizabeth Markham
Born May 12th 1836

Thomas
Markham
Died
Oct^{br} 22nd
1826

Mary Ann
Markham
Died
Novr 20th
1833

Worked by S Stearn

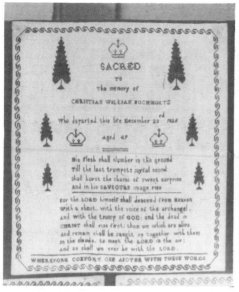

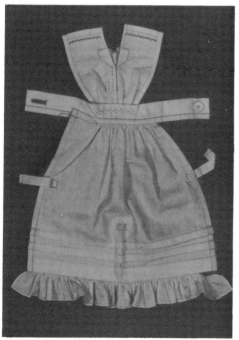

ABOVE LEFT: *Circa 1825; English; black silk on linen. One of a set of three samplers worked by Louisa Buchholtz, aged thirteen, mourning the deaths of both her father (1825) and mother (1823). The other two are identical except for names and dates, while this one is larger, a little more elaborate with a more cheerful verse. (Norfolk Museums Service, Strangers Hall Museum 332.965)*

ABOVE: *1901; English; signed 'EKMI' and dated; cotton thread on evenweave canvas. Sampler bound with ribbon showing plain sewing stitches, darning button-holes and the attachment of tapes. The stitches are all exaggerated in size and would be used for teaching. Worked for the City and Guilds examination in needle-work. (Norfolk Museums Service, Strangers Hall Museum 67.970.4)*

LEFT: *1901; English; signed 'EI'; coloured thread on lawn and calico. Sampler showing many processes as well as stitches and leaving part unfinished to show methods of working. (Norfolk Museums Service, Strangers Hall Museum 67.970.4)*

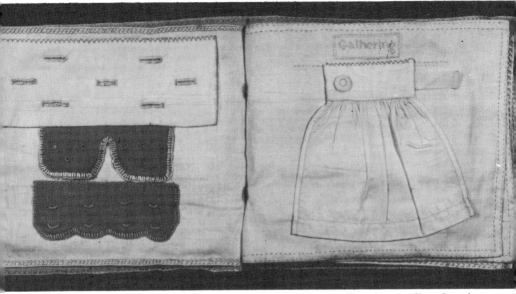

Late nineteenth century; English; cotton and silk threads on flannel and calico. Sampler in book form with all the usual processes shown and each page edged with feather stitch. (Victoria and Albert Museum T67-1967)

PLAIN SEWING SAMPLERS

During the nineteenth and early twentieth centuries unpretentious samplers of plain sewing were very common. They started in the charity schools and orphanages and were later embodied in the curricula of the schools of domestic science and needlework, especially in the City and Guilds examinations. Although many homes had a domestic sewing machine after the 1860s dresses and underwear were still frequently made by hand and a knowledge of stitches and processes such as tacking, gathering and inserting gussets was essential.

STITCH SAMPLERS

By the end of the nineteenth century decorative samplers worked by children had become completely stereotyped and were poor in both design and technique. However, the sampler was too useful an exercise to disappear completely; it took a new form showing stitches and ways to use them rather than patterns and designs, and it is in this form that it is most commonly used today.

1919: English; signed 'AGIC' and dated; linen threads on linen. Worked by the well-known needlewoman and teacher Mrs Archibald Christie for her book 'Samplers and Stitches', showing composite stitches. (Victoria and Albert Museum 1919)

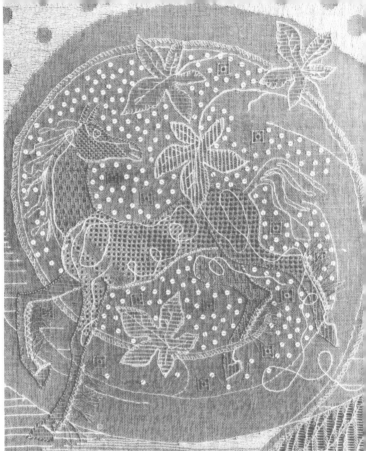

ABOVE LEFT: *1930s; English; coloured stranded cottons on linen. Detail of long sampler showing methods of building simple stitches into patterns, with edging, insertion and filling stitches. Worked by Muriel Dawbarn. (Norfolk Museums Service, Strangers Hall Museum 2.972.9)*

ABOVE RIGHT: *1938; English; linen threads on linen with sequins. Worked by Rebecca Crompton illustrating pulled fabric stitches. This sampler comes close to the rather vague line which divides samplers from embroidered panels. (Victoria and Albert Museum C218-1948)*

RIGHT: *1965; English; coloured crewel wools on canvas with twenty-four threads to the inch. One of six sections of a folding book illustrating canvas stitches. Each design is worked twice showing alternative treatments. Worked by D. Harmer. (D. Harmer collection)*

KIT SAMPLERS

The twentieth century, while still continuing with the old traditions of sampler-making, has seen one big innovation, the marketing of samplers ready designed, often with the necessary threads included – the kit samplers. These generally commemorate a national happening or illustrate something which appeals to a number of people who may not have the skill, the inclination or the time to design for themselves.

ABOVE: *1977; English; coloured wools on canvas. A kit sampler designed by Anna Welbourne and marketed by the National Trust, illustrating one of their properties.*
OPPOSITE: *1937; English; designed by Miss Aldous. The spring 1937 number (61) of 'The Embroideress' included three coronation samplers and one illustrating the jubilee of King George V in 1935. The transfers could be bought and the fabrics and threads were indicated.*

Sixteenth century; Italian; coloured silks on linen. Random designs with characteristically flowing patterns. These are obviously patterns collected for future use and there are far more than appear at first sight.(Victoria and Albert Museum T14-1931)

SOME FOREIGN SAMPLERS

Countries of the world with a high standard of needlework have their samplers which reflect the style most generally seen there. Also nuns, usually from predominantly Catholic countries, have through the centuries taken their skills to developing countries, where there appears a type of sampler showing characteristics of both the new and the parent country.

1758: Danish; signed 'Rebeckea Asgni' and dated; linen thread on linen. A beautiful sampler with ninety-six different patterns of drawn and pulled work. The late eighteenth century was a period when dress accessories such as aprons, handkerchiefs and ruffles were often exquisitely worked on the finest muslin. Denmark had a tradition of superb whitework as this sampler proves.(Victoria and Albert Museum T27-1940)

LEFT: *First half of the sixteenth century; German; coloured silks on linen. Random patterns, very formal in outline. Some of the motifs are obviously going to be used on altar linen and include the Crucifixion, Instruments of the Passion, Pelican in its Piety, the Sacred Monogram and various crosses. (Victoria and Albert Museum T114-1956)*

BELOW: *1870; Mexican; signed 'Virginia Samtibañes' and dated; coloured silks on linen. A late sampler from Mexico showing strong European influence and an interest in drawn thread work. Most of the designs could be of a much earlier date, especially the S motifs, which can be seen on many seventeenth century samplers. (Victoria and Albert Museum T288-1928)*

Eighteenth century: Dutch; signed 'Lannette Maas'; coloured silks on linen. A sampler which is very similar to English work, except for the Dutch lion enclosed in a hedge and the interest in the four Delft vases. The motif 'the return of the spies from Canaan' seen in so many English samplers is here shown three times. (Victoria and Albert Museum T11-1937)

31

PLACES TO VISIT
Intending visitors are advised to find out the opening times before making a special journey.

Blaise Castle House Museum, Henbury, Bristol BS10 7QS. Telephone: Bristol (0272) 506789.

Broughton House, High Street, Kirkcudbright, Scotland. Telephone: Kirkcudbright (0557) 30437.

Cambridge and County Folk Museum, 2/3 Castle Street, Cambridge CB3 0AQ. Telephone: Cambridge (0223) 355159.

Fitzwilliam Museum, Trumpington Street, Cambridge CB2 1RB. Telephone: Cambridge (0223) 69501. (Possibly the finest collection in England.)

Gawthorpe Hall, Padiham, Burnley, Lancashire BB12 8UA. Telephone: Burnley (0282) 78511.

Hove Museum of Art, 19 New Church Road, Hove, East Sussex. Telephone: Brighton (0273) 779410.

Nottingham Museum of Costume and Textiles, 51 Castlegate, Nottingham NG1 6AF. Telephone: Nottingham (0602) 411881.

Old House Museum, Cunningham Place, Bakewell, Derbyshire.

Rufford Old Hall, Liverpool Road, Rufford, Lancashire L43 1FG. Telephone: Rufford (0704) 821254.

Strangers Hall Museum, Charing Cross, Norwich, Norfolk NR2 4AL. Telephone: Norwich (0603) 611277 extension 275. (Good collection with many plain sewing and twentieth-century examples.)

Victoria and Albert Museum, Cromwell Road, South Kensington, London SW7 2RL. Telephone: 01-589 6371. (An excellent collection with many foreign examples.)

Wells Museum, 8 Cathedral Green, Wells, Somerset BA5 2UE. Telephone: Wells (0749) 73477.

Whitby Museum, Pannett Park, Whitby, North Yorkshire YO21 1RE. Telephone: Whitby (0947) 602908.

Whitworth Art Gallery, University of Manchester, Whitworth Park, Manchester M15 6ER. Telephone: 061-273 4865.

FURTHER READING
Colby, Averil. *Samplers, Yesterday and Today*. Batsford, 1964.
Dreesmann, Cecile. *Samplers for Today*. Van Nostrand Reinhold Company, 1972.
Huish, Marcus B. *Samplers and Tapestry Embroideries*, London, 1913.
Jones, Mary Eirwen. *British Samplers*. Pen-in-Hand, 1948.
King, Donald. *Samplers*. HMSO, 1960.
King, Donald. 'Boxers'. *Embroidery* volume XII, number 4.

ACKNOWLEDGEMENTS
The author gratefully acknowledges the help given by Miss S. M. Levey of the Victoria and Albert Museum; Miss Barbara Schnitzer of the Fitzwilliam Museum; Miss Fiona Strodder of Strangers Hall Museum; Mrs June Dalton, who drew the stitches; Mr Andrew Paton, who took the photographs on pages 2, 5 (right), 11, 14, 16, 18, 19 (bottom), 20 (left), 22, 25 (top left and bottom); Mr A. Snowdon and Mrs D. Harmer, who lent samplers; Messrs. Pearsalls Ltd, who allowed publication of one of their prints; and the National Trust, who photographed and allowed publication of one of their kits. Permission to reproduce photographs of samplers in their collections was kindly given by the Victoria and Albert Museum, Strangers Hall Museum, the Fitzwilliam Museum and Bewdley Museum.